BATMEN

NIGHT AIR GROUP 90 IN WORLD WAR II

By

John W. MacGlashing

ISBN: 1-883809-08-8

Text by John W. MacGlashing
Illustrations by John Valo

Published by:
Phalanx Publishing Co., Ltd.
1051 Marie Ave. W.
St. Paul, MN 55118-4131 USA

European Distribution by:
Air Research Publications
P.O. Box 223, Walton on Thames
Surrey, KT12 3YQ
Great Britain

FRONT COVER: A General Motors assembled Grumman TBM-3D of VT(N)-90

REAR COVER: The insignia of VF(N)-90 was carried on their Hellcat fighters. It was rendered for the squadron by the famed cartoonist, Milt Caniff.

Printed in the United States of America

DEDICATION

This history is dedicated to all those personnel who did not return from their cruise on the U.S.S. ENTERPRISE, CV-6 the most decorated ship of World War II. Out of twenty-one battles, the BIG E was in twenty of them. It was a sorry day in our history when the Congress of the United States allowed this ship to be scrapped.

An unknown seaman was heard to say "She is a ship with a soul", and after my service on her, I firmly believe this.

It is also dedicated to Lieutenant Commander Robert J. Mc Cullough, Lieutenant Nelson V. Phillips, of VF(N)-90, both of whom I respected and admired greatly, and Lieutenant Russell Kippen, the first C.O. OF VT(N)-90 whom I knew only for a short period of time but found to be a great officer.

John W. MacGlashing

ACKNOWLEGEMENTS

History of VF(N)-90 1945 (declassified)
History of VT(N)-90 1945 (declassified)
THE BIG E by CDR. EDWARD P. STAFFORD
Personal Diary of FRANKLIN GOODSON, Member of VF(N)-90
Personal Diary of ROBERT ROY, Member of VT(N)-90
Personal Diary of WAYNE THOMPSON, Member of BIG E
Deck logs of the U.S.S. ENTERPRISE (CV-6) (declassified)
Action Reports COMMANDER NIGHT AIR GROUP NINETY (declassified)
NITE LITE VT(N)-90 PAPER

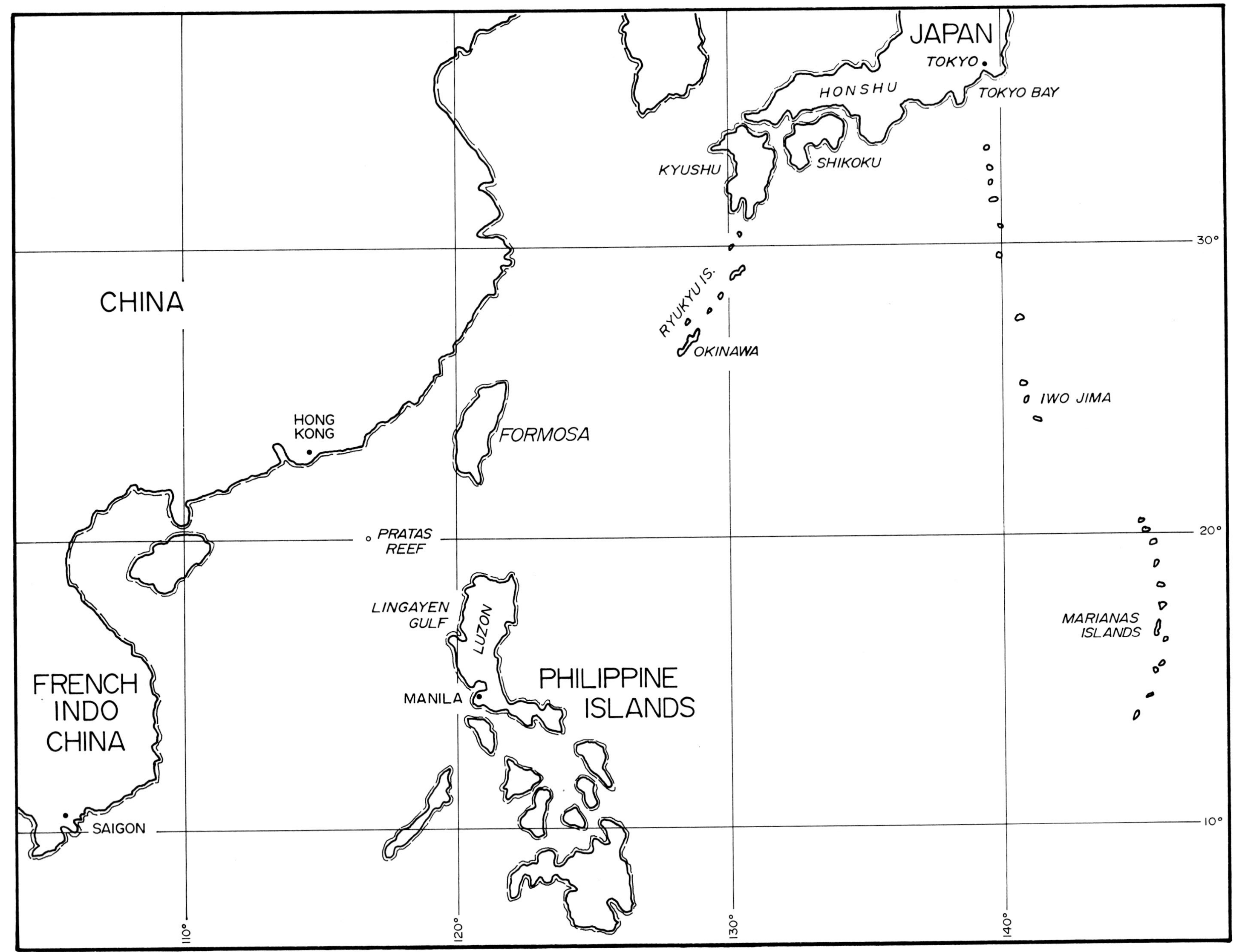
JAPAN
TOKYO
HONSHU
TOKYO BAY
KYUSHU
SHIKOKU
CHINA
RYUKYU IS.
OKINAWA
IWO JIMA
HONG KONG
FORMOSA
PRATAS REEF
LINGAYEN GULF
LUZON
MARIANAS ISLANDS
FRENCH INDO CHINA
MANILA
PHILIPPINE ISLANDS
SAIGON
30°
20°
10°
110°
120°
130°
140°

General Motors built Grumman TBM-3D Avengers of VT(N)-90 had its AN/APS-3 radar mounted under a pod on the leading edge of the starboard wing. The turret and tunnel machine guns were also eliminated, but wing mounts for 5 inch rockets were added. They carried two wing mounted .50 caliber machine guns. (Credit: Bill Balden)

EARLY CARRIER NIGHT OPERATIONS

When war came to the vast Pacific Ocean, it would revolve around aircraft carrier strike forces. Yet in 1942 the U.S. Navy had no night combat operating syllabus, and such exercises would have been considered reckless. Japanese night tactics soon compelled a change in procedures.

Lieutenant Commander William I. "Bill" Martin, along with the legendary Butch O'Hare and others, had long been thinking of night flying from a carrier as a way to counter enemy snoopers. In October 1942 Martin was C.O. of VS-10 aboard the USS *Enterprise* and submitted a proposal to utilize a single plane reconnaissance unit equipped with radar. Shortly thereafter VT-10 received one Grumman TBF equipped with ASB-1 radar, and Martin was given the opportunity to develop its potential along with Lieutenant Henry Loomis the ship's radar officer. They recognized its capability, as well as its limitation, but this was the seed that started the development of night carrier operations.[1]

Authorization was received in mid-1944 to form the first air group in Naval history that would do 85 to 90% of its flying at night. [2] In August 1944 Night Air Group 90 was formed under the leadership of Commander Martin to employ his theories.

Up to this time night flying was used mainly as a defensive tool, Combat Air Patrol (CAP), and engaging any enemy that wandered in or near the fleet after being picked up by radar. This is not to say that many of the night fighter squadrons already in the Pacific theater did not engage in offensive action. The new concept was unique because it was the first time it would be utilized both offensively and defensively.

In February 1944, VT-10, led by Martin, had staged a night attack on Japanese shipping in the harbor of Truk, and each plane in VT-10 had scored more then one direct hit on various targets. This showed that night flying could inflict severe damage on the enemy, and be utilized as an offensive tool. This type of raid was made possible with the use of radar that Martin and Loomis had developed in 1942. Ironically, Martin did not participate in the raid due to an accidental injury received aboard ship, and Lieutenant V. Van Eason was assigned to lead thirteen TBFs on the mission. Only one plane failed to return.

VF(N)-75 was one of the first night fighter groups to enter combat, and they were split up into four detachments. One of these detachments became VF(N)-101assigned to Air Group10. The original night fighters were F4U Corsairs flown by Navy pilots. VF(N)-101was commanded by Lieutenant Commander R. E. Harmer, and he is credited with the first radar-intercept splash of a bogey by a carrier based night fighter on April 24, 1944. VF(N)-20 was another of the detachments from VF(N)-75, and it served with Air Group 20.

These two night fighter outfits are noted as they were assigned to air groups whose primary function was daylight combat, and the primary mission of the night fighters was protection of the fleet at night. In August 1944 VF(N)-79, then on its way to the combat zone, was implemented with a torpedo plane complement, and it, in reality, became the first night carrier air group to enter combat, but was utilized both as night and day, not strictly as a night group.

On April 5, 1944 VF(N)-103 was commissioned under the command of Lieutenant Commander Robert J. Mc Cullough. He had been serving on the USS *Belleau Wood* as Fighter Director Officer. The author, John

Members of VF(N)-103 who were incorporated into VF(N)-90 shown here at Charleston, RI in April 1944. (L. to R.) Dick Jones, R.A. Davis, Joe Parela, Jim Purcell and Bob Wright (MIA). (Credit: MacGlashing)

"Speed" Mac Glashing, Yeoman Second Class, was serving in the Pacific in a Carrier Aircraft Service Unit when ordered to report to VF(N)-103 at Quonset Point Naval Air Station in Rhode Island.

A bond was created between the "skipper" and the author that lasted until 1982 when Mc Cullough passed away. In my opinion and that of many others in the squadron, he was the type of officer you would follow to hell and back. Within hours after the formal commissioning at NAS Charleston, several pilots arrived. Then the enlisted personnel started to check in. Lieutenant Nelson V. Phillips reported on board as Executive Officer. A strange coincidence was that both the skipper and exec attended Springfield College, both graduated in 1938 but had not previously met.

The original complement called for twenty-five officers and twenty-one enlisted, but later when VF(N)-103 became VF(N)-90 the complement was changed to forty-two officers and fifty enlisted. Some of the new personnel we received when VF(N)-90 was formed came from VF(N)-104 and VF(N)-106 also trained at Charleston, so most of the personnel knew each other, which made for a smooth transition.

The first few days after commissioning of 103 was devoted to checking personnel in as they arrived, and checking over the aircraft, twelve F6F3-Ns equipped with AIA radar .

Training started in earnest about April 8, 1944. It consisted of tactics, gunnery, carrier landing practice, and the rest of the syllabus required of day fighters, but the big difference was it was all done at night. Of necessity pilots learned instrument flying, and became most proficient at its use. The thing most peculiar to night fighters was the use of radar, and it occupied a large portion of the training period. The men soon became used to doing everything at night. The toughest part was sleeping during the day as the remainder of the base was on a day schedule. Midnight meals were

Left side of a VT(N)-90 TBM pilot's cockpit shows the position of the radar (only the scope is seen) just right of the throttle controls. (Credit: Bill Balden)

Looking forward in the Avenger cockpit the pilot's radar screen is just visible (absent the scope) in the lower left (Credit: Bill Balden)

meager, and served by a skeleton crew! The twelve and fourteen hour shifts were tough, but much had to be accomplished in a short period of time. The only major casualty during training was the loss of Ensign James P. Gannon of New Jersey killed in an accidental crash of his plane near Shantuck,Rhode Island. During the end of the training period the pilots checked out on carrier landings aboard CVE's *Mission Bay* and *Tripoli* .

Avenger pilot's cockpit, right side. (Credit: Bill Balden)

Skipper of Night Air Group 90 was Bill Martin, shown here between his two crewmen during a prior tour of combat when he commanded VT-10. (Credit: Bill Balden)

Up to that time the pilots had been making simulated landings on a portion of the runway set aside for that purpose, even using Landing Signal Officers, and no runway lights so they could experience a night carrier landing, in the middle of a dark ocean. Four months later, August 5, 1944, VF(N)-103 departed for NAS, San Diego. The sixteen pilots who were flying the F6Fs across country gave NAS, Charleston a buzzing that would not soon be forgotten. They advised us later that a couple of the personnel in the tower were ready to bail out as they thought the F6Fs were coming right through. A letter of reprimand was awaiting the squadron when it arrived at San Diego.

NIGHT AIR GROUP 90 FORMATION

Prior to the change in orders received in August 1944, it was set up so that four Grumman F6Fs, six pilots, and a supporting team would be a detachment aboard a single carrier. There would have been four groups in all, aboard four different carriers. No one in the squadron was looking forward to this arrangement, as they had become a very close knit bunch in the previous four months, and felt that esprit de corps would be lost.

However, just before leaving Charleston it was decided that we would be one undivided unit when we arrived at Pearl Harbor. On the evening of August 7, 1944 all of the planes arrived in San Diego except for Ensign Jim Purcell who had been forced down at NAS Floyd Bennett Field in New York with engine problems. Jim showed up on August 9th. To this day it is suspected that Jim was happy to be forced down in his native New York.

A transport plane brought the remaining pilots, some officers, and some enlisted personnel. As much as we loved flying, sitting in bucket seats cross country in a prop driven aircraft isn't much fun. The rest of the enlisted personnel and officers arrived by train. On August 10th all of the gear was stored on a CVE, the USS *Rudyard Bay*, and on August 17th we arrived at Ford Island, Pearl Harbor. A lot of the men had not previously been to Pearl Harbor, and the scars of 7 December were still visible.

On arrival we were ordered to Barbers Point Naval Air Station, and our orders showed we would be part of Night Air Group 90. It was further learned that we would be assigned to USS *Enterprise* (CV-6) which then would become CV(N)-6 devoted exclusively to night operations. On arrival a week or so later VF(N)-104 and -106 were decommissioned, and became part of VF(N)-90. On August 25, 1944 VF(N)-103 was decommissioned and VF(N)-90 was established.

Night Air Group 90 was born without a complement of torpedo planes, and on September 24th Commander William I. Martin arrived taking over as CO of the air group. With him came fourteen officers from VF-10, plus enlisted personnel from VT-10. As of that moment the entire purpose of night flying changed to both defensive and offensive with a new training syllabus. Lieutenant Russell Kippen became The CO of VT(N)-90. Kippen had been one of the pilots from VT-10 that had participated in the first offensive night attack, the Truk strike of February 17, 1944.

Radar interception was still an important part of the training. Radar mast head bombing was scheduled and practiced and CAPs by the Hawaii based aircraft were flown over carriers regularly. It was during this training that the use of picket destroyers, to increase radar range, was developed. At regular intervals field carrier landings were held followed by actual day and night carrier landings on the USS *Ranger* and USS *Saratoga*. A significant change from previous training was the requirement of visual identification before firing on the bogie. The requirement practically eliminated the use of radar gun sights.

On September 30th a complement of thirty-two fighters was established, sixteen F6F-5Ns equipped with AN/APS6A radar, and sixteen F6F-5Es equipped with AN/ASPA (ash) radar gear. Training for VT(N)-90 was accomplished almost entirely with borrowed TBM-1C type aircraft. A few TBM-3Ds were available during the latter part of training, and in December1944 nineteen

A pair of Hellcat fighters of VF(N)-90 on a dusk mission carry auxilliary fuel tanks. (Credit: Bill Barr)

of the assigned twenty-seven TBM-3Ds were received by the squadron. Toward the end of training the fighters and torpedo planes were equipped with rocket launchers, and that rounded out the group's arsenal.

During the training period the fighter group lost two of their pilots. On August 31, 1944 Ensign Richard B. Jones of Grand Rapids, Michigan crashed into the sea just south of Waikiki Beach. On November 10, 1944 Ensign John F. Lungershausen of Culver City, California while on a practice mast head bombing run crashed into the sea about a mile off the coast of Oahu. The torpedo group lost six men: On October 15th Ensign James J. Murphy of Hartford, Connecticut flew into the side of a mountain during night training on Oahu. He was alone at the time of the unfortunate accident. Then, on October 18th Ensign Charles W. Barton, Bronx, New York , and his crewmen James C. Hayes of New London, Connecticut and Kenneth H. Ramsey, Richmond, California crashed into the sea about 100 miles off the coast of Oahu. Ensign James L. Crane of Hillsboro, Indiana and his crewman George M. Herlofsen of Aberdeen, South Dakota crashed into the sea 150 miles off Oahu on October 20th.

On the brighter side of the training period, a beach party was held for the officers at the Outriggers club at Waikiki, and was attended by Admiral Matt Gardner who was 100% behind this new concept of night flying. A beach party was held for enlisted personnel at Nimitz Beach a fleet recreational facility. Also a short R&R was given to air group personnel on the Island of Hawaii where they stayed at the Volcano Kilauea (house of everlasting fire). An everlasting "thanks" to the torpedo bomber pilots who graciously ferried the personnel to the island, and returned for them two days later.

Enlisted members of VF(N)-90 at a Hawiian beer bash. (L. to R.) Charles Brubaker, John McNerney, Evan Willis, John Colligan and Joe Hrosak. (Credit: MacGlashing)

This echelon flight of VT(N)-90 TBM-3Ds provide a good view of the wing mounted radar unit pod. The photo was taken near Hawaii. (Credit: Bill Barr)

The *Enterprise* underway from Pearl Harbor. (Credit: MacGlashing)

CHRISTMAS EVE 1944

The BIG E returned to port around the end of November, and on December 17th orders were received for Air Group 90 to report on board. The feats of the venerable ship were known to every sailor in the Navy, and we were proud to become part of its heritage. On Christmas Eve at 1500 hours the *Enterprise* shoved off, slid down the east channel of Pearl Harbor, through the sub nets, her bow turning to the west. About 1700 hours the air group appeared on the horizon, Avengers flying in the shape of an "E" and Hellcats in the shape of a "V", symbolic of the two letters that were synonymous "*Enterprise* and victory".

All planes landed safely, and as evening set in so did the realization that it was Christmas Eve and that we were going out to do battle. Everyone tried to stay busy and not talk or think about it, but it was tough.

INITIAL CASUALTIES AT SEA

From operations log USS *Enterprise*: 26 December 1944:

> "Today one VF(N) and VT(N) crashed on take off. Radioman of VT(N) was lost and all other personnel were rescued with no serious injuries. A VF(N) made a hard landing on deck which carried away its belly tank. The tank was cut by the propeller and started a fire on deck which resulted in superficial damage to the flight deck, major damage to the plane, and burns to personnel which resulted in the death of one man, severe burns to one man, and moderate burns to two officers and five enlisted men".

The VT radioman was Nick Curnice, ARM3C of Chicago, Illinois. The pilot was Lieutenant (j.g.) Robert R. Jones, Hawthorne, Georgia, and the other crewman was Carl D. Jones, ARM3C of West Virginia.

> Message received: 27 December 44 from: COM Third Fleet "Let us dedicate this Christmas to the unshakeable resolve that we will leave nothing undone, to hasten by crushing of aggression, the return of peace on earth and to secure the lasting peace on earth that Christmas symbolizes. We can rejoice that our homes and families are safe and now let's get on with the war. Halsey"

During afternoon of 29 December a TBM spun in during approach for landing.

The pilot, Lieutenant (j.g.) Eugene Ralph Lee of Portland, Oregon was lost. But both crewmen, Robert L. Lundfe, ARM3C from Renora, Pennsylvania, and Armando Nelso, AOM2C from Los Angeles, California were saved.

We sailed in a routine manner until January 5, 1945, and made our rendezvous with Task Force 38.5 under the command of Rear Admiral Matt Gardner. Ad-

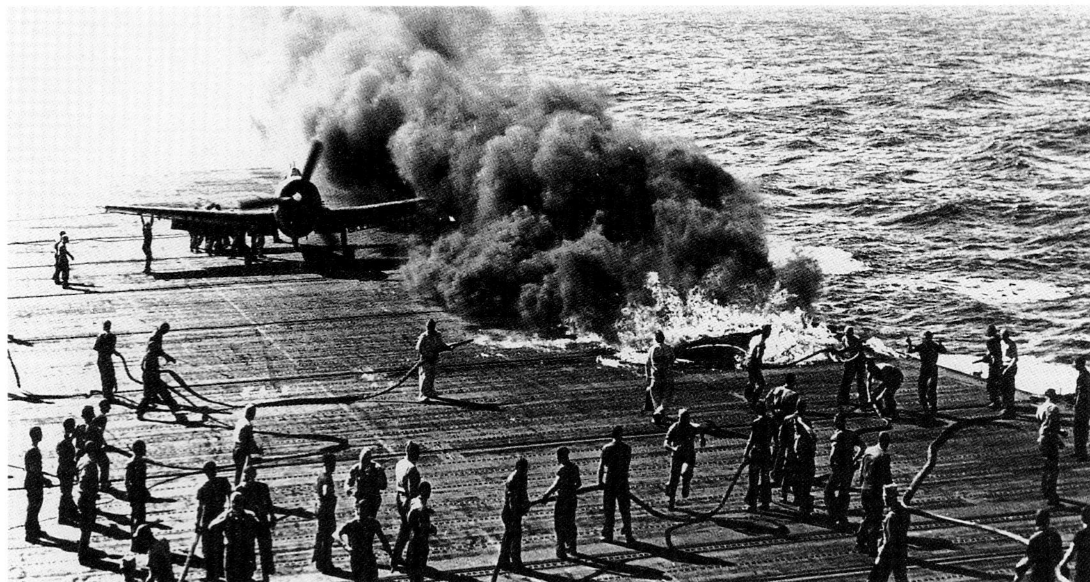

The belly tank of an F6F breaks loose on landing and starts a deck fire on *Enterprise*. (Credit: Bill Barr)

miral Gardner had previously commanded the BIG E in 1943, and was its CO when Martin's VT-10 made the first night attack against Truk. Captain Grover B.H. Hall was the current commanding officer of *Enterprise*.

Message received from: COM, Third Fleet Action: COMCAR Div 7 *Enterprise*

> "MSG Admiral Gardner, staff COMCAR Div 7, officers and men of *Enterprise*. With great pleasure I welcome COMCAR Div 7 and his staff to the Big Blue team and I am happy to have the *Enterprise* back in her regular position. From past experience I know we can expect great things from the galloping ghost. Halsey"

Admiral Gardner took command of the Fifth Task Group within Task Force 38. This group, which was the first night carrier task force group in the history of naval operations, consisted of *Enterprise* and *Independence* along with six destroyers.

FIRST ENGAGEMENT

The long awaited return to the Philippines had occurred in October 1944 with the invasion of Leyte. Mindoro had been invaded the following December, and by January the stage was set for General Douglas MacArthur's forces to conduct amphibious landings in Luzon's Lingayen Gulf. Navy support for Philippine operations had been massive and ship losses had been heavy primarily due to the advent of the first concentrated Kamikaze attacks. *Enterprise* reentered the war at this point, launching her first offensive strike in support of the Lingayen invasion.

The first night operation was sent off at 0430 on January 7, 1945 against Clark Field, Luzon, the Phillippines with fifteen fighter planes being catapulted from 235 miles at sea. Only twelve planes reached their target as three had radar difficulties. The twelve that hit the area assigned were met by heavy anti-aircraft fire, but no enemy planes.

All returned safely to the BIG E, but Lieutenant Commander McCullough, the CO of VF(N)-90, had to land with most of his controls shot up, and hydraulic system out. His plane crashed through the barriers, and went over the side by the port gun mount forward of the ship. I was standing on the island outside the Air Officers position, and seeing this occur broke down assuming he had been killed.

It was the author's job during landings to check off the planes as they returned, so I knew immediately that it was the skipper. Luckily he was picked up by a

Skipper of VF(N)-90 Lt. Cdr. Robert J. McCullough. (Credit: MacGlashing)

plane guard destroyer following behind, and was returned to the *Enterprise* with repairable injuries.

Also during the strike, Ensigns "Sandy" Latrobe and "Keg" Kegelman received AA damage to their planes. While ensuing fire from the skipper's crash was put out, and minor repairs made, the remainder of the aircraft landed aboard the *Independence*.

As would be the case for both VF and VT in future engagements, much of the damage incurred could not be precisely assessed, though in this engagement it was believed that severe damage had been inflicted on aircraft and installations at Clark Field.

At 1500 on January 7, 1945 a four plane strike was launched on targets in northern Luzon. Lieutenant Carl Nielsen drew first blood for the air group by shooting down three enemy aircraft, a Dinah, Oscar and Zeke.

Another eight-plane fighter sweep over Lingayen corridor and Clark Field was launched simultaneously. One Zeke was destroyed at Clark, a truck load of Japanese soldiers was strafed, and rockets fired into a factory and railroad yard. The weather became very heavy with very poor visibility, and on return Ensign Charles "Gibby" Gibson, of Philadelphia,Pennsylvania, and Ensign John Sowell of Kernshaw, North Carolina collided in mid-air. Sowell was able to get over the fleet and probably bailed out as the USS *San Diego* reported seeing flares, but no rescue was accomplished.

Also at 1500 hours, a night heckler was launched consisting of four torpedo planes. Lieutenant Charlie Henderson and Lieutenant (j.g.) "Gibby" Blake hit Aparri and Laoag Airfields starting a fire at the latter. Lieutenant Joe Doyle and Lieutenant (j.g.) Cliff Largess hit Aparri and Palaui and reported the phrase that would become familiar "damage unobserved because of the darkness".

The following day VT(N)-90 planes were launched to try and locate downed fighter pilots. A bit of humor came out of this flight when "Gibby" Blake found his plane had been "sabotaged". When attempting to use the relief tube he found it missing. He learned that a glove was not a good substitute.

SOUTH CHINA SEA

On January 9, 1945 the task force entered the South China Sea. This was the first time since hostilities began that a naval force other then submarines had entered into this area. Admiral Halsey believed that some of the enemy battleships which survived the Battle of Leyte Gulf were in the region.

Night searches were launched on the 10th into very adverse weather conditions, but nothing was found, and on the 11th more night searches but still no Japanese fleet. Around noon on the 12th a convoy was sighted which consisted of five destroyers, and escorts. The torpedo group reported one patrol vessel probably sunk, one destroyer seriously damaged, one patrol craft and one destroyer strafed causing explosions. Ensign Jim Landon and Ensign Joe Jennings were later awarded DFCs for their part.

The fighter group, led by Lieutenant Nelson Phillips, the XO, followed by Lieutenant (j.g.) Logan MacMillan, Ensigns Dick Jones, Stan Kurant, Lamar Harrison, and Frank Truhowsky, reported direct rocket hits with explosions on two destroyers, two patrol vessels and two destroyer escorts. Ensign Truhowsky, on his run, had his oil line hit, and made a water landing. An OS2U was dispatched from the USS *Pasadena* and under fighter protection by Lieutenant Commander McCullough and Lieutenant Carl Nielsen the Kingfisher was able to land and recover Truhowsky, who was found uninjured.

On January 13th, Lieutenant. Russell Kippen, CO of the torpedo group, led part of his squadon against a light cruiser. Later this cruiser, the *Kashi*, was found to be beached and sunk. At 1550 hours a fighter group consisting of Lieutenants Phil Horr, K.D. Smith, O.D. Young, Lieutenant (j.g.) Hettwer, Ensigns Campbell, Woods, Gille and Lockwood made an attack on Saigon #7 airfield destroying 9 enemy aircraft, plus three probables, and one damaged.

At 1700 a three-plane fighter sweep was launched led by Lieutenant James J. Wood, with Ensigns Sandy Latrobe and Robbie Robison. They attacked Saigon Airfield, shot rockets into a patrol craft

Lt. Nelson Phillips, Executive Officer of VF(N)-90 and unknown plane captain. (Credit: MacGlashing)

and destroyer escort, destroyed a Betty and a Topsy on the ground at Tan Son Nhut field and set several oil storage tanks on fire. On the 13th and 14th night searches were dispatched with no success, as the weather deteriorated. One of the searches by TBMs went all the way to Hong Kong.

On the 13th Ensign John B. Heddons of VT(N)-90 was coming in for a landing, crashed and went into the sea. His crewmen John Hotchkiss and Robert Brought were picked up with him, but Brought succumbed to his injuries on the 17th. Our luck was getting worse on losing personnel.

A typhoon was now 200 miles south of the Task Force. On the 15th Captain Hall launched a strike of torpedo and fighter planes to destroy a weather/radio station on Pratas Reef. The air group Commander Bill Martin led the mission consisting of eight Avengers and four Hellcats. Russ Kippen CO of VT(N)-90 and Bob Mc Cullough CO of VF(N)-90 were members of the attack unit. The installation was heavily damaged and an Oscar on the ground set on fire. The weather became so bad that the strike had to return by flying on the deck just above the water. Lieutenant (j.g.) Shannon McCrary crashed into the sea moments after being catapulted. He escaped and was rescued but his two crewmen, Mervin Porter ARM3C and Manford Cooney ARM1C were not so fortunate.

On 16 January at 1630 hours four fighters were launched over Hong Kong and Canton. One Tojo was shot down by Ensign Bob Wattenburger with an assist by Lieutenant James Wood. A power house, radio tower, warehouse and radar station were strafed or rocketed.

Returning from the mission Ensign Erwin G. Nash of Philadelphia, crashed into the sea just aft of the ship and was not recovered. At 1750 hours a four plane night fighter heckler mission was launched over Hong Kong and Canton. Various installations were shot up with rocket fire and strafing. Lieutenant (j.g.) Robert Wright of Athens, Georgia did not return and was listed as missing. Heavy AA fire was met over Hong Kong, and the weather was atrocious with huge waves breaking over the bow of the *Enterprise* making landing and launching treacherous.

Out of eight planes dispatched that day one disappeared, one crashed into the sea, two hit barriers, and one landed with wheels up. The old quote, "War is Hell" was uncomfortably realistic.

Bob Wattenburger, shown here as a 22 year old ensign. (Credit: Wattenburger

Japanese installations on Pratas Reef being pounded by Air Group 90. (Credit: Bill Balden)

On January 20 and 21 attacks were launched on the air fields of Toko Heito and Eiko on Formosa. Damage again could not be determined but many blazing fires were observed.

On January 21 two fighter planes and one Avenger were launched against Tainan airfield at Formosa. The operation was led by Lieutenant James Wood. The torpedo plane developed engine trouble before reaching the target area, so one Hellcat returned as escort. Lieutenant Wood continued to the target alone so moved into the traffic pattern over the airfield where Japanese planes were landing, picked off a twin-engine Frances bomber, let his rockets go into a line of aircraft on the ground, and quickly moved out of the area.

Tokyo Rose had predicted over the radio that the fleet would not leave the China Sea alive, but in Admiral Halsey's words, "We made a liar out of Tokyo Rose again". We passed safely through the Bashi Channel out of the China Sea during the night of January 21. At one time we were under attack by Japanese planes, but no serious damage was done.

Early on January 22nd a seven-plane torpedo strike on Kiirun, Formosa led by Commander Bill Martin was launched. Shipping had been reported in the harbor at Kiirun. Ensign Hinrichs had to return to the ship because of engine problems. Lieutenant Russell Kippen, CO VT(N)-90, led a three plane flight consisting of Lieutenant (j.g.) Chester G. Koop and Ensign John Wood. Each of the planes carried a 500 pound bomb, plus three rockets under each wing. As they entered the target area search lights stabbed the sky. Kippen was heard over the speakers in air combat to say he was being blinded by the lights as he made his run, and that AA was very heavy. No more was heard from this flight after that transmission.

Commander Martin led the second flight in with his crewmen Lieutenant Commander William B. Chase, radar observer, and Robert Barrett, ARM2C. He was followed by Lieutenant (j.g.) Joseph Jennings with his crewmen William Albert Griffin, ARM2C and Peter G. Smith, AMM2C and Lieutenant (j.g.) William Cromley with his crewmen Leonard Prym, ARM2C and John G. Murphy, AMM2C.

The attacks netted one small cargo ship destroyed with numerous fires on the wharf and water front. Searches were subsequently made for the Kippen trio, with no luck. Lost along with Kippen were his crewmen Lieutenant (j.g.) Uri Alexander Munro, and Paul Adrian Floyd, ARM1C; Koop, his crewmen Guy Beevers, Jr., AMM2C, Dale Albert Lieberenz ARM3C; and Wood, his crewmen John Howard Findley, ARM3C, and Richard James Hall, AMM3C.

On January 22nd, four Hellcats led by Lieutenant Owen D. Young, with Ensigns Wallace Campbell, John Kenyon and Charles Latrobe were launched at 1630 hours over Naha Airfield on Okinawa. Damage again could not be assessed because of darkness, but some fires were seen on departure.

While returning to Ulithi for replenishment on January 25th Ensign Knox O. Scott had a landing accident. His tailhook caught a wire but his Avenger went over the side breaking in half. The tail remained on deck, but the rest went into the water. Ensign Scott and his crewman Eugene A. Wengle, ARM3C escaped and were picked up. They tried to rescue the other crewman, Dennis Crowley, ARM3C, but the plane sank too quickly.

Enroute to Ulithi the chaplain held memorial services for the lost members of the ship's crew and the air group. It had been a tough first month. In addition to the

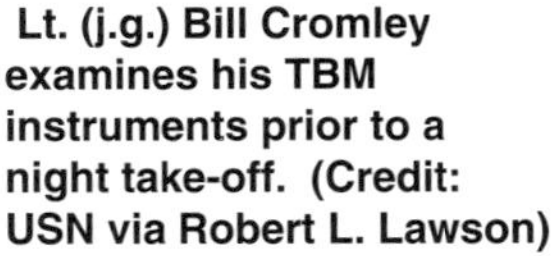

Lt. (j.g.) Bill Cromley examines his TBM instruments prior to a night take-off. (Credit: USN via Robert L. Lawson)

strike missions air crews flew CAPs over the fleet at night, and also the day when the weather was too foul for the day fighters. No night interceptions were attained, as the Japanese kept their planes pretty much away from the fleet. The weather in the South China sea was atrocious, with the ship rolling and pitching, making take-offs and landings nearly impossible. At times the sea and sky literally met.

An outfit that works at night and tries to sleep during the day has its problems. The barber shop, ships store, etc., kept day hours, so it was difficult at best to get to these departments while they were open. It would seem that we would just be getting to sleep when not under attack, when you would hear that familiar call, "Sweepers man your brooms, clean sweep fore and aft". However, the ship's crew and officers did their best to make us feel right at home, and individually and collectively they were most cooperative.

ULITHI

On January 26, 1945 in a low overcast and a persistent drizzle, we entered Ulithi lagoon where we would stay until our sortie on February 10th. Most of the time was devoted to recreation. Basketball and volleyball were held on board ship. Motion pictures were available every night as were numerous beach parties. VT(N)-90 kept torpedo planes at the airstrip on Fallalop for anti-sub patrols, and miscellaneous duties. Each pilot and crewman spent at least one or two days there from January 26th until they flew back aboard *Enterprise*. During the beach parties on Ulithi the enlisted personnel voted unanmiously that the trip to the beach was not worth the limit of three (3) beers. Some of the more enterprising enlisted personnel were able to obtain extra rations, as a few were seen to return aboard somewhat less then sober. I'm not going to tell who (hic), but (hic) one was a yeoman and a few aviation radarmen, aviation radiomen, aviation mechs, etc. The best part was receiving mail that was not weeks and weeks old. Even some Christmas gifts arrived.

JAPAN HERE WE COME

Admirals Halsey and McCain had returned to Pearl, and Admirals Spruance and Mitscher were back operating Task Force 58 with whom we sortied. The BIG E became part of 58.5 with Admiral Matt Gardner flying his flag from *Enterprise*. The *Independence* was replaced by the Saratoga. The battle cruiser *Alaska*, heavy cruiser *Baltimore*, light cruiser *Flint* and nine destroyers made up task group 58.5.

Our direction was northeasterly, and then it was announced that we were headed for Japan. At 1830 hours a CAP of eight fighters was launched returning at 2200 hours. During the landing Ensign William Leroy Sadler of Portland, Oregon in taking a wave-off, caught his tail hook on the LSO cage, stalled out and dropped into the sea, With the plane upside down rescue ships could not locate him. Lieutenant Ray Tenant, the Landing Signal Officer, had to leap for his life to keep from being struck.

Fighter pilots, (L. to R.) Lamar Harrison, Nelson Phillips and K.D. Smith ice the Budweiser Lager beer for a Ulithi party. (Credit: MacGlashing)

An Avenger goes over the edge on landing but the crew made it out. (Credit: Bill Balden)

We sailed north, east of Guam and between the Nampo-Shoto Islands and Marcus Island, arriving off the Japanese coast before dawn on February 16th. General quarters was sounded at sunrise. This was to be an historic event because it was the first "all Navy" air strike against Tokyo. In April 1942 *Enterprise* had escorted the *Hornet* when they launched General Doolittle and his B-25's on their attack on the Japanese mainland. On February 16, 1945 at daybreak, the day fighters and other aircraft were catapulted for the initial attack against enemy installations. At 1615 hours twelve fighters from VF(N)-90 were launched for a patrol to hit airfields in and around Tokyo to prevent counter attacks by the Japanese against the fleet. It was led by Lieutenants Russell D. Otis, Kenneth "K.D." Smith, and Owen D. Young. They were followed by Ensigns Stanley Kurant, Francis "Tex" Luscombe, John Kenyon, Kenneth Close, Charles Latrobe, Arthur Hansen, Glen Earl, James Tucker, and Fred Hunziger.

On take-off Ensign Francis Luscombe hit the water, was seen grabbing onto his belly tank but just as the destroyer pulled alongside he apparently lost his grip due to severe injuries, and sunk out of sight. All losses were great, but this one seemed to have an effect on all hands, as "Tex" was a friend to everyone who came in contact with him. "Tex" had gone on liberty with several of us together in Rhode Island, and he showed us how to pick up girls Texas style.

The weather at launch time was very poor with a solid overcast from 500 to 2,000 feet with icing conditions above 3,000 feet. Over the targets it was clear. The planes reached the coast of Japan at Yamata Saki, turned southwest and followed the coast line around the tip of Chiba peninsula directly across from Tokyo Bay, to Tateyama.

Seeing nothing there the flight proceeded up the bay to Yokosuka, and at this point they broke into three divisions. As they entered the Yokosuka vicinity all of the planes came under heavy intense AA fire, which lasted until they left.

Division one was led by Lieutenant Otis followed by Ensigns Hansen, Earl and Hunziker. They were the first to go in, strafing a row of twin-engine and a row of single-engine aircraft destroying several. Ensign Earl then spotted a ship in the bay and proceeded to strafe same while salvoing his rockets. The action caused an explosion aboard the enemy vessel. While he was moving out of the area a Zeke made a run on him, but Earl immediately gave his F6F full power leaving the enemy aircraft behind. In the meantime Ensign Hunziker had been hit and forced to make a water landing near the fleet, and shortly after was picked up by the destroyer *Longshaw*.

Division two was led by Lieutenants Smith and Young followed by Ensigns Latrobe and Tucker. Coming in from a different direction they strafed and sent rockets into an enemy airfield. Four freighters proceeded to fire on them, and were strafed in return. They then proceeded out to the coast and to Choshi, strafing and firing rockets at airfields. Continuing northwest they strafed a radio tower, three railway locomotives, a radar station and factory.

Division three led by Lieutenant (j.g.) Logan Mac Millan with Ensigns Kurant and Kenyon, flew close cover for the other two divisions while they were hitting airfields. Ensign Kenyon found a Mitsubishi J2M, Jack fighter on his tail, and MacMillan came to assist him, and the enemy aircraft broke off. At about this time, Kenyon found another Jack heading straight at him. They exchanged gun fire, but neither plane apparently received damage. The Japanese pilot broke away from the formation as Kenyon tried in vain to get behind him.

Shortly after all fighters were launched, a torpedo plane manned by Lieutenant Charlie Henderson, with Lieutenant (j.g.) Ted Halbach and Henry Loomis operating the electronics gear, were sent out to jam Japanese radar. One Hellcat was sent along as an escort.

On February 17th shortly after midnight, an eleven torpedo plane night search and attack group was launched. The target was part of the island chain 150 miles south of Tokyo Bay. Hachijo Jima and Nii Shima were searched and their airfields attacked. There was no sighting of the Japanese fleet, and damage to the airfields was unconfirmed because of the darkness, but fires were seen blazing as they left the area.

On return to the ship Ensign John Whitney Stuckey flew into the water apparently from vertigo. An accompanying plane searched the area, dropping flares and dye marker, but no survivors were seen. Nor was there any sign during a subsequent daylight search. The two Crewmen were Victor George Channey, AOM3C, and James Clark Eldred, ARM3C.

VF(N)-90, limited to CAPs, though Tokyo was again under attack. That evening we went through Nampo straits leaving the Tokyo Area, and early on February 19, 1945 took our position off Iwo Jima.

It was D-Day as dawn found U.S. Marines beginning one of the toughest island invasions of the Pacific war. The next four days the usual CAPs were flown. On February 19th Lieutenant James Wood was vectored onto a bogie, made a positive identification and shot down one Ki.49 Nakajima, Helen heavy bomber. That made Jim's record one Dinah and one Helen.

On the 22nd we joined the Seventh Fleet to take the place of the Saratoga which had been hit by kamikazes. The BIG E was now the queen of the jeep carriers. Our job as part of Task Force 52.2.5 was to provide night coverage for the fleet supporting the Iwo Jima invasion. TBMs were launched into skies with ceilings below 500 feet to search for pilots from the "Sara" who were missing.

A division led by the CO of VT(N)-90, Lieutenant C.B. Collins broke through the overcast over some of our ships during a "red" alert. Spooked by kamikaze attackers, someone was quick on the trigger and slow

A Japanese Army Ki-49 Helen bomber of the type encountered during Iwo Jima operations. (Credit: Jim Lansdale)

on recognition and opened fire on our planes. The rest of the ships also opened fire and the skipper's plane was hit, and last seen losing altitude and smoking. Ensign Henry G. Hinrich's plane was also badly hit, and in spite of heavy fire from the fleet he made a successful water landing. He and Michael C. Ryan, ARM3C escaped injury, but crewman Everett H. Caswell, AMM2C was wounded, and was assisted from the plane by Hinrich and Ryan. A small subchaser nearly ran them down, as its crew was manning the siderails with small arms pointing at the three Avenger personnel. Ensign Hinrich's loud, continuous, and explosive use of the "American" invective convinced the crew that they were not Japanese, so much so, that the skipper of the craft jumped into the water to aid in their rescue.

The loss of the second skipper of VT(N)-90 was depressing. Lieutenant Collins' crewmen were Lieutenant (j.g.) Robert J. Gowdy, and Ferris Ivory, ARM2C. Lieutenant Charles Henderson was appointed the new Commanding Officer, and the new Exec was Lieutenant James Stanley Moore, Jr.

During the early morning hours of February 22nd Lieutenant Commander Bob McCullough, CO of VF(N)-90, and Lieutenant Owen Dewitt Young were officially credited with breaking up an air attack on the fleet by Japanese planes. They had been vectored onto a number of bogies, and on making positive identification, engaged them. Surprised at the presence of the American Navy nighters, the enemy bombers aborted their attack and fled into the darkness.

ALL TIME RECORD

On February 23, 1945 at 1630 hours, VF(N)-90 began what turned out to be an all time record for continuous flying from a carrier. It is unknown if that record has been broken by prop driven aircraft, but possibly with today's modern aircraft it has. Night and day our pilots flew night CAPs, day CAPs, target CAPs, sweeps and intruder missions over Chichi Jima and Iwo Jima. Hour after hour the flights went on and the aircrews began to tire, as they had two flights and a standby condition in one twenty-four hour period. Day after day the record continued until March 2nd at 2330 hours when the total continuous hours amounted to 175.

The first ninety-nine hours forty minutes of this record passed without a serious deck accident until Ensign Rex Milton brought his plane in striking gun mounts and the island on the starboard side. His plane broke into three distinct pieces, and he emerged without serious injury. VF(N)-90 had averaged fifty flights every twenty-four hours. Forty-five minutes after the record ended our planes were in the air again flying sweeps over Chichi Jima and CAPs over Iwo Jima, until March 10th when we were relieved to return to Ulithi. While the record was being accomplished VT(N)-90 was also busy. On February 23rd they searched, without success, for Lieutenant Collins and his crew.

NAG 90 aircraft action reports of February 24, 1945 show six planes from VT(N)-90 were launched at 1530 through 1625 over airfields at Chichi Jima and targets of opportunity at Chichi and Haha Jima. Lieutenant Charles Henderson led the flight with his crewman Lieutenant (j.g.) Edwin Halbach and ARM2C Thomas "Tex" Henderson. Also included in the mission were Lieutenant (j.g.) George E. McLaughlin with his crewmen, ARM3C Ellwood Littlefield and AOM1C Philip Morgan; Lieutenant (j.g.) Charles Gerbron with his crewmen ARM3C Edward Cobb and ARM3C Thomas Armstrong. Lieutenant (j.g.) William Balden with his crewmen ACMM Lee Sturla and ARM2C James Kitchen; Lieutenant (j.g.) Bob Heid with crewmen ARM2C Arnold Rouse and ARM3C Charles Baker; and Lieutenant (j.g.) Ralph Turpin with his crewmen ARM1C Harry Shaw and ARM2C Oliver Ohlund. Lieutenant (j.g.) Gibby Blake and Ensign Rob Roy had to return because of mechanical failure to their planes.

The formation flew due north to a point east of Haha Jima where Balden and Heid separated for an attack against shipping and other targets. The primary target at Chichi Jima was Susaki airfield. Balden and Heid made their first glide bombing run from north to south on the town of Omura. Eighteen frag clusters struck a concentration of small buildings which extend approximately 600 feet from the harbor front and started fires. The only shipping observed was three barges in the harbor at Okimura.

At Susaki airfield Gerbron and McLaughlin hit two single-engine planes and a Betty bomber. Lieutenant Henderson dropped six frags on wharves and buildings in Omura with unobserved results. He then made a run on a ship lying in Susaki inlet with four rockets being released two of these seen to explode at the bow about ten feet above the water line. Lieutenant (j.g.)Turpin aimed six frags and six rockets at this target also with unknown results.

McLaughlin and Heid each obtained rocket hits on two supply ships lying in Futami harbor near the naval installation. Gerbron threw a long burst of .50 caliber bullets into one of the several important radio stations at Chichi. The accuracy of well exercised Japanese gunners was thoroughly confirmed. Gerbron's port wing was hit by automatic fire as he was making a run on the airfield. Despite a marked flutter in all his tail surfaces he was able to return to base.

On the 26th six planes on radar patrol and six on pre-dawn sortie hit Chichi Jima. The airstrip at Chichi was attacked with unobserved results. Lieutenant James S. Moore's plane was hit during the attack, and he was forced to make a water landing east of Chichi. He and his crew, radar operator Lieutenant (j.g.) Robert B. Hadley and ARM1C Thomas T. Watts were found by Lieutenant Joseph Doyle and he vectored a rescuing destroyer to them. Tom Watts had been trapped inside the plane, and was freed by Bob Hadley who went to his aid, at risk to himself. Hadley was awarded the Navy and Marine Corps medal for his rescue of Watts.

On the afternoon of February 24th Ensign Robert M. Woods of VF(N)-90 was hit by ack-ack fire over Chichi Jima, and forced to ditch about forty miles off shore. Ensign George E. "Ben" Franklin stayed with Woods until relieved by a team of Commander Bill Martin in a TBM, and an escorting Hellcat. Woods was picked up by the destroyer *Paul Hamilton* and returned to *Enterprise*.

Lieutenant Phillip Horr, with Ensigns George Lockwood, and Pete Taylor of VF(N)-90 pressed their attack on Chichi Jima. Anti-aircraft fire was immensely heavy. At 1815 hours Lieutenant Kenneth "K.D." Smith, flying a lone wolf patrol, spotted a Helen bomber over Chichi Jima, came in from behind, opened fire and followed the twin-engine aircraft down to the water where it exploded.

During the period of February 19th through March 9th, heckler missions, night CAP, photo missions, etc., were flown over Iwo Jima and Chichi Jima by both squadrons. On March 8, 1945 the Navy command wanted some hand delivered messages taken to the Marines on Iwo Jima. Lieutenant (j.g.) Cliff Largess, who had a Marine brother stationed at Iwo, ferried Lieutenant Commander Ward of the flag staff onto the island. While Ward delivered his message, Cliff located his brother and had a nice visit.

On March 9th Lieutenant Commander Frank Belcher issued a special newscast to the *Enterprise* crew as follows:

> "A party of officer-observers from the *Enterprise* visited Iwo Jima yesterday on March 9th and returned to the ship with souvenirs and first hand accounts of the battle for the island as it stood on the 19th day since the Marines' initial landing on 19 February. The southern airfield on which we landed, had already been lengthened and graded. We were amazed at the activity on this field, where a surprising number of Army fighters were seen.[3] There were a number of marine TBFs, Navy and Army transports, with PB4Ys, and even a B-29 on the field. In fact, there was such an enormous amount of air activity going on over and on Iwo, it was hard to understand why the remaining Japanese, dug in such a short distance away, hadn't decided to call it all off and give up. Around the field were wrecked Zekes, Bettys, and other Japanese aircraft in quantity still laid in heaps where they were hit or have been pushed aside."

The story goes on, but ends with this:

> "They are still fighting on Iwo Jima. The dust and dirt and living conditions the men over there have to put up with made those of us from the ships feel a little embarrassed to think of our comparative luxury. But they are not complaining, and are finishing up the job they started. They're very grateful for the air support during the past three weeks, and grateful to the *Enterprise* pilots for keeping enemy raiders "off their necks" at night time. While they may not know it yet, its a pretty safe bet that when it's all over, this victory will prove to be one of the most important of the entire war in hastening the final end."

FINALLY, GOOD SHOOTING

Operation ICEBERG, the invasion of Okinawa, an island just 340 miles from Japan, was slated for April 1, 1945. In preparation for that historic assault, and in anticipation of a violent reaction by Japanese air units based in the home islands, the fast carriers focused on Kyushu.

"Old No. 64" lands long and hot missing all the wires. (Credit: Bill Balden)

Avenger 64 has just come to rest among the parked TBM and F6F aircraft on *Enterprise*. (Credit: Bill Balden)

A closer look at the damage. (Credit: Bill Barr via MacGlashing)

After resupply at Ulithi we sortied with Task Force 58 on March14th, 1945. There was very little flying by the air group until March 18th when at midnight three fighters were launched for CAP over Kyushu, with eight torpedo planes being launched for intruder mission over Kyushu, and an attack on the city of Kagoshima.

Lieutenant (j.g.) Ralph W. Cummings led a group of six over these areas doing considerable damage to radar installations and railroads. The unit included Lieutenant (j.g.) William L. Cromley, Lieutenant (j.g.) George W. Bruel, Ensign Knox O. Scott, Lieutenant (j.g.) William R. Thomas, and Ensign Robert Roy. Lieutenant Joseph Doyle with his wingman Lieutenant (j.g.) Joseph M. Scarborough struck three major airfields in eastern and southern Kyushu starting many fires.

During the CAPs the hunting was extraordinary. Lieutenant (j.g.) Bob Wattenburger was vectored onto a bogie, and chased it all over the western Pacific through clouds, around the fleet, into rain squalls one after another, but finally it paid off with one Helen splashed.

Lieutenant (j.g.)Wesley "Doc" Williams chased a bogie for almost three hours, through rain squalls and away from the fleet, and finally knocked down an unidentified single-engine Japanese plane. Lieutenant (j.g.) Jim Purcell encountered a Tabby twin-engine transport and after a long chase fired on same striking the port engine which burst into flames and caused the DC-3 replica to crash. Ensign Glen Earl found a twin-engine Frances in the clouds after being vectored by a picket destroyer. He fired and the plane burst into flames as he followed it down to the water. Lieutenant (j.g.) Will Squires, after strafing a Japanese picket boat, spotted a Jake float plane and splashed same.

Layton Robison (right) with unknown plane captain. (Credit: MacGlashing)

The only casualty of the long night was Lieutenant (j.g.) John W. Cole, shot down by friendly fire and rescued by a destroyer. Again, a case of too quick on the trigger before identifying the plane, but the fleet had been under heavy attack most of the time from the Kamikazes.

The pilots who were not on flying duty received a rude awakening at approximately 0730 when it was announced over the P.A. system that an unexploded bomb had struck the #1 elevator. The officers bunking area was just forward of the elevator, so needless to say those still in their quarters made a fast exit. The 550 pound bomb was a dud but did cause some damage. Later in the torpedo squadron ready room, after another attack by a Kamikaze, someone mentioned that it seemed cold and did anyone else notice it. Bob Heid was heard to remark, "I don't know about the temperature but this trembling I'm doing ain't from patriotism."

On the 19th the torpedo squadron made an attack in the Inland Sea and reported one cargo vessel probably sunk, two seriously damaged, and one destroyer escort seriously damaged. The pilots causing the carnage were Lieutenant (j.g.) Shannon McCrary, and the VT(N)-90 CO Charlie Henderson.

In the meantime, Lieutenant Ernie Lawton made the discovery of the night, a carrier and a battleship within three miles of each other. He and his crew dropped their 500 pound bombs on the carrier, and sent their remaining rockets into the battlewagon. Damage could not be confirmed due to extreme darkness.

An Emily flying boat was intercepted by Lieutenant Charlie Henderson and shot down by him and his crew.[4] Damage was inflicted on installations at Kurashik, Mitsubishi Mishima plant and Soeki airfield by Lieutenant (j.g.) Bill Balden and Lieutenant (j.g.) L. "Torr" McLaughlin.

During the morning of the 19th, Lieutenant (j.g.) S. Lamar Harrison and Layton Robison teamed up on a Mitsubishi Betty bomber sending it to Davy Jones' locker. At the same time Ensign James R. Perkins ran into another Betty and fired into the port engine which burst into flames. He pursued it through clouds until ordered to cease the chase as the enemy bomber headed toward Japan, still burning.

On March 20th seven torpedo planes made an attack on airfields on the Islands of Kyushu and Shikoku. One unidentified plane was intercepted and shot down by Lieutenant (j.g.) Cliff Largess and his crew. There were large fires and explosions among the ground installations, but definite results could not be determined. The pilots involved in this raid were Lieutenant Jim Moore the XO, Lieutenant Ralph W. Cummings, Lieutenant (j.g.) Gilbert "Gibby" Blake, Ensign James Landon, and Ensign Henry "Gordo" Hinrichs.

The fleet had been under heavy attack for four

Don Hettwer, VF(N)-90, and unknown plane captain. (Credit: MacGlashing)

Bob Corbit of VF(N)-90 with unknown plane captain. (Credit: MacGlashing)

days March 18th, 19th, 20th and 21st. On the 19th the *Franklin* and *Wasp* were both hit. The *Wasp* damage was controllable, but the *Franklin* had been hit hard. It was sickening to watch it burn from the deck of the *Enterprise*. VF(N)-90 flew CAPs over her until she was able to move under her own power on the 20th. After the fires were brought under control the cruiser *Pittsburgh* took her in tow and the BIG E assisted her out of the danger zone.

On the 20th while escorting the *Franklin* a Judy began to stalk the *Enterprise*. He finally came in and dropped his 500 pound load, a tremendous explosion that missed by about fifty feet. Lieutenant (j.g.) Rob Roy of VT(N)-90 noted the incident in his diary:

> "I was on the flight deck as the next enemy plane approached. He was s-turning high above us at 8 to 10,000 feet. He then pushed over coming for us. I watched all the ships shooting at him, but he kept coming. I decided to go to the ready room to take cover. I waited tensely expecting this plane to crash into the ship when I felt a sudden shudder and I realized a bomb must have been dropped.
>
> "I went back onto the flight deck again and learned a bomb had gone off on the starboard quarter in the water. The plane, a Judy, was flying away taking evasive action. There was a cloud of smoke on the flight deck under "Fly Control". Several F6Fs were on fire. Planes were being moved aft away from the fire, and I jumped in an F6F and worked the brakes while crewmen pushed it back. Ammunition was beginning to explode so I took cover in the port catwalk."

Five-inch cross fire was bursting across the deck, and one projectile, equipped with an influence type fuse detonated over an *Enterprise* 20mm battery killing two men, and wounding four more.

The *Enterprise* seems engulfed by the damage from a March 20, 1945 Kamikaze, but thanks to her gallant crew she lived to fight another day. (Credit: USN via Ken Cashen)

A closeup view of damage on *Enterprise's* flight deck (above and below) caused by the March 20th Kamikaze as fires are brought under control. (Credit: Bill Barr via MacGlashing)

A General Motors assembled Grumman TBM-3D of VT(N)-90. Radar was carried in the pod on the leading edge of the right wing. Besides the pilot there were two other crew members.

Grumman's highly successful F6F Hellcat, was the premiere Navy fighter of World War II. VF(N)-90 operated both the -5N and the -5E which were identical except for the radar unit mounted in a pod on the right wing.

Before departing the fleet for repair and resupply we had to leave twelve fighter pilots with other carriers. Those who volunteered were Lieutenants Russell D. Otis, Kenneth "K. D." Smith, Owen D. Young; Lieutenants (j.g.) Logan Mac Millan, John Cole, William Piscopo, Richard Jones, Stanley Kurant, John Kenyon, and Charles Latrobe; also Ensigns James Tucker, and Joseph Sowar.

During that interim period "K. D." Smith of Port Arthur, Texas and Bill Piscopo of Los Angeles, California accounted for three confirmed and one probable kill between them. Waldo West of Crown Point, Indiana splashed three bandits by himself. All of these kills were at night.

On March 24th the *Enterprise* anchored back in Ulithi Atoll. A successful beer party was held on the beach for the enlisted personnel, this time with enough beer for all hands.

OKINAWA – KAMIKAZE JUNCTION

We departed on April 5, 1945 to rejoin task group 58.2 and arrived on April 7th to support the invasion of Okinawa. On a day patrol Lieutenant Dallas Runion and Lieutenant (j.g.) Rex Milton joined forces to send a Frances to a watery grave. The torpedo group sent two night hecklers over nearby airfields. Again, because of weather and darkness damage could not be observed.

On the 9th the torpedo group launched night hecklers over Japanese Ryukyu airfields, again with results unobserved. On that same night Lieutenant (j.g.) Will Squires of VF(N)-90 splashed a Val that was making a run on one of our destroyers. Squires pressed his attack ignoring his own danger and followed the Val through anti-aircraft fire from the destroyer exhibiting unusual qualities of courage and valor.

On the 11th Lieutenant R. W. Cummings of VT(N)-90 while on a night strike at airfields in the Ryuku chain intercepted a Tabby transport and with his crewmen, Zane Carey and Joe Lindsey, splashed same. Large gasoline fires were seen by the planes from VT(N)-90 that had hit airfields. In the early morning Dallas Runion VF(N)-90, while returning from an unsuccessful Bogie chase, ran into a single-engine Kawasaki Tony and downed it.

The fleet was under heavy attack by the Japanese on the 11th. The first plane to come after the *Enterprise* was splashed by its gunners. A while later a Kamikaze hit the port quarter forty millimeter battery, killing several of the gun crew and doing a lot of structural damage. About thirty minutes later another Kamikaze was dropped into the sea a few feet from the ship. The bomb this plane was carrying went off causing more structural damage and setting afire an F6F on the catapult. Ensign Franklin T. Goodson wrote in his diary for April 11th:

> "Today was another red letter day. We were calmly watching a movie in the ready room when reports came that two groups of enemy planes were heading for our task force. The movies were shut off and the pilots began to man their planes.
>
> "At 1400 hours our planes were catapulted and the fireworks began. One Kamikaze dove for the *Enterprise* amidst the spray of antiaircraft fire. We swerved and he missed diving into us and crashed into the water so close to the stern that it blew a hole in the ship bursting an oil blister. We trailed oil but nothing real serious developed. Two men were blown overboard, but I believe they were picked up by our destroyers. Pieces of the Japanese plane fell on our flight deck.
>
> "At 1430 another Japanese Zeke Kamikaze made a dive at our deck. He hit the plane on the starboard catapult setting it on fire and shearing off his own wing. The rest of the enemy plane went over the side and into the water. The *Enterprise* crew shot down six aircraft which tried to sink us. Watching the seventh plane being shot down, I was almost hit by shrapnel. The plane came in high and was hit twice. It burst into flames and came streaking down crashing and scattering its parts everywhere.

A near miss by a Kamikaze on April 11, 1945 set fire to a Hellcat on *Enterprise*. (Credit: Bill Barr via MacGlashing)

A Japanese Army Ki-67 Peggy bomber was encountered and downed over the Ryukyus by Jim Wood. The aircraft pictured was from the 107 Hiko Sentai. Bearing a close resemblance to the Betty, this aircraft was designed by Mitsubishi and built jointly by Kawasaki and was the best of Japan's "heavy" bombers. (Credit: USMC via Jim Lansdale)

"Eleven crew members were injured, two very seriously. A Japanese communique was intercepted, and our intelligence officers report an all out attack against us today and tomorrow. Tonight they are dropping flares and hunting for us....having no success In locating us they reported to their base that they could not find us and told the air group that was to relieve them to return to base."

During the early morning of April 12th K. D. Smith of VF(N)-90 chased a Betty all around the fleet. He dropped back when the task force opened fire on the enemy bomber then resumed the chase as it left the fleet. He was finally able to close and destroy the enemy aircraft. Lieutenant (j.g.) Joseph Gallant during his CAP was vectored onto a twin-engine Japanese bomber, a Betty or a Peggy. After overshooting it a few times, he finally closed, and opened fire, sending the plane into the water where it was seen to explode. Shortly after this encounter Joe Wood intercepted and downed a Peggy.

Ensign James R. Perkins, after being vectored in the general vicinity of a bogie, caught a Jake dropping a flare, chased it and on a maneuvering turn, fired a deflection shot that sent it crashing into the extreme northern tip of Okinawa.

In the meantime VT(N)-90 had an eleven plane night heckler mission going over airfields in the outlying islands. Many fires and explosions were seen by the crews of the torpedo planes.

On April13th the death of President Franklin Roosevelt was announced to solemn crew members of the *Enterprise*.

The same day Ensign Fred Hunziker of Clewiston, Florida was reported missing. He had been on the tail of a Betty and last reported they were low over the water, then nothing further was heard. We were ordered to return to Ulithi for repairs on the 14th, but again left fourteen fighter pilots and three aviation radar techs behind to help in the battle against the Kamikazes. Those volunteering were Lieutenant James Wood, Lieutenant (j.g.)s Frank Truhowsky, Robert Wattenburger, Robert Corbit, James Purcell, Joseph Gallant, Donald Hettwer, Richard Jones, Rex Milton, Robert J. Smith and Ensigns Edward Kryshak, Waldo W. West, James R. Perkins and Franklin Goodson. The ARTs were ART1C William Mc Kinney, ART1C Robert Linfield and ART1C Leon H. Gary. The fighter squadron had hoped to remain intact until its return to the states, but the desperate situation around Okinawa prevented this.

On April16th the officers of the air group and the BIG E held a farewell dinner for Rear Admiral Matt Gardner who had been transferred. On the 17th orders came to transfer fighter director officers Lieutenant Ray Weathers and Ensign R. I. Rodemyer to ships company. On the same date fighter director officers John E. Toffolon and Leonard Wilmoth were permanently transferred to the picket destroyers from which they had been working.

THE PERILS OF THE NIGHT

Night fighting was patently perilous, but when the mission was over the terror for the flight crew had not ended. They had to seek out their blackened ship in a dark sea and then land aboard an often pitching deck.

Carrier landings in broad daylight, in the best of weather are considered a hazardous undertaking. At night landing problems are magnified beyond comprehension. With the frequent absence of horizon, stars or moon, vertigo — a trick of the inner ear that suggests imbalance — plagued night aviators.

Taylor Caldwell, a veteran of VF(N)-41 flying from *Independence*, was quoted as saying: "Flying off a carrier is dumb. Night flying is even dumber."

Bill Balden, a veteran of both VT-10 and VT(N)-90, who logged 1,133 hours of flight time, 124 carrier landings and 16 night landings, describes the "thrills" involved in a night launching, and the subsequent carrier landing.

"The nights were most always really black, often with cloud ceiling of 300 to 500 feet. I'd often sit in the cockpit and hope, 'Maybe they'll recognize it's too damn bad to fly tonight.' But I'd get the 'throttle up' signal and off we'd go. We were catapulted off the deck at 65 knots. If you didn't fly your instruments, in the drink you'd go! All was well once you were leveled out with wheels and flaps up.

"We would generally take two hours to the target, two hours there on a heckler mission, and then two hours back.

"On returning to the *Enterprise* there was a problem of finding what to land on. We could pick up the fleet with our radar, but upon arrival all that was visible was the white wakes of the ships on the water. The only light visible was one 360 degree red light on the carrier. The problem was finding this red light. When we located it we would pass along side going the same direction as the ship at 300 feet. This altitude and heading were maintained for one minute, then came a 90 degree left turn for one-half minute, then a 90 degree left turn to head back toward the carrier while gradually letting down to 150 feet.

"When we were alongside the carrier we would be picked up by radar and instructed to start our third turn. This was a gradual turn getting closer to the water. At this point my knees would often tremble with my feet on the rudder pedals.

"When behind the ship, the deck lights would be on and we could soon pick up the Landing Signal Officer. This was a big relief, for he would tell us what to do on the approach. After all of this there was one thing we didn't want to have happen — a wave off!

"To me this phase of night carrier flying was the most hazardous thing a Navy pilot could ever experience. It is really a miracle that any of us survived!"

The pilot's perspective of night operations was somewhat different than that of the crew in the rear of a TBM Avenger. Joe Hranek, an ARM1C on Gib Blake's plane, provides this recollection from his position in the tunnel or the rear turret:

"The catapult shot was a real thrill, especially if everything wasn't tied down. Once there was a scope cover left loose, and as the plane surged forward it shot backward and skinned my forehead. After that I checked more carefully to make sure everything was 'tied' down.

"During flight operations I had my eyes glued to the windows if I wasn't on the radar. On one occasion in the tunnel I spotted a glow that I couldn't identify and told Blake about it. He must have been too busy to answer, and besides he knew it was the exhaust of another of our planes. I thought it might be a Jap sneaking up on us until they moved and I saw the profile of the plane. Your view wasn't as distorted from the turret.

"On landings I would watch the water coming up and record the altitude. But was never sure where we were until he cut the engine and the deck lights suddenly appeared. All in all it was sheer terror."

Lt. (j.g) Bill Balden in the "office" of his night Avenger. (Credit: Balden)

Cutting a cake to mark the 45,000 landing on *Enterprise* are (L. to R.) Charles Henderson, VT(N)-90 CO, Bill Martin, CAG, Bob Jones and Bill Balden. (Credit: Bill Balden)

The squadron insignia of VT(N)-90, shown here, was not carried on their aircraft. The artist was Roy Pintacura. (Credit: MacGlashing)

An Avenger of VT(N)-90 lies upside down in the water after a landing accident. Although only one crew member is visible, all survived. (Credit: Bill Balden)

THE FINAL CAMPAIGN

A beautiful shot of Avengers of VT(N)-90. (Credit: Bill Balden)

On May 4th, 1945 *Enterprise* left Ulithi after extensive repairs to the ship, to rejoin Task Force 58 for what would prove to be her last campaign.

At 0300 on May 7th we launched eight fighters. Four departed for airfields in the Ryukus and four flew a CAP over Okinawa. The airfield flight section did some damage with Lieutenant Runion and Ensign Goodson reporting they shot up a radio station very badly. Neither flight engaged any enemy aircraft.

At 1730 four more fighters were launched over Kikai Shima and they reported finding two Francis on the runways, destroying both.The following day we received the welcome news that Germany had surrendered unconditionally. At 0345 on May 9th four fighters were launched over Kikai. On take off Lieutenant (j.g.) James T. Tucker of Rockford, Illinois crashed into the sea off the port bow. He became the eleventh and final fighter pilot to lose his life. The remaining planes patrolled the area where Tucker had gone down, but found nothing and returned.

Admiral Marc Mitscher comes aboard *Enterprise* in a breeches buoy, his previous flagship, *Bunker Hill*, having been hit by a Kamikaze. (Credit: Bill Balden)

A flight of Grumman Hellcats of VF(N)-90 at dusk. The squadron employed both F6F-5E and N models. (Credit: Bill Balden)

Night Air Group 90 encountered many Aichi E13A float recon aircraft known to the Allies as the "Jake". The unit shown here was conducting ASW training operations off the coast of Japan in 1944. (Credit: National Archives via Jim Lansdale)

At 1730 hours four more fighters were launched over Amami O Shima and Kikai. They shot rockets and strafed airfields with results undetermined. On the 10th a ten torpedo plane night heckler was launched over Ryukyu airfields but results could not be determined.

On the 11th a nine torpedo plane night heckler was launched over Kyushu's Kanoya airdrome complex and again results could not be determined. Also on this date we welcomed aboard Admiral Marc A. Mitscher and *Enterprise* became the flag ship of the task force. It had been quiet since our return to the fleet, too quiet. All hands sensed that something must be brewing from the Japanese.

With the situation for the Japanese on Okinawa now desperate, coupled with the May 8th collapse of their ally, Nazi Germany, the Special Attack Corps (or Kamikaze) determined to hurl ever greater strikes against the Allied fleet.[5]

The night of May 12th the task force hovered within striking distance of Kyushu and the Northern Ryuykyu Islands. At 0230 a fighter patrol of seven planes was launched, proceeded to Tanega Shima, split up and covered the various fields. Again hunting was good. Lieutenant Owen D. Young spotted the exhaust of a plane, made a positive visual identification and on his second pass shot down a Tony fighter.

K.D. Smith was on a strafing run when he found his controls were jamming, so decided to return to the ship. On the way home he was surprised to see tracer bullets passing him, looked around and found two Tony's on his tail. Despite his control problems he was able to maneuver his plane until he got behind one and downed it. The other Japanese retreated as did Smith.

Lieutenant Young in the meantime found some Jakes flying low over the water, and in ten minutes splashed three of them. As he joined up on his wingman

A Hellcat of VF(N)-90 makes an approach to *Enterprise* in a sky marred by fleet anti-aircraft fire. At right center the LSO, paddles upraised, is showing the pilot that he is high. (Credit: MacGlashing)

Miyazaki Airdrome, shown here in a high altitude recon photo, was an important Japanese airfield on the East coast of Kyushu. It was a target of Night Air Group 90 and a launching point for attacks on Task Force 58. (Credit: USN via Balden)

Lieutenant (j.g.) Charles "Sandy" Latrobe, they spotted a Pete float aircraft, both fired and scored again. Lieutenant (j.g.) John Kenyon chased an Oscar for seven miles, finally catching and splashing the Japanese fighter.

That same night VT(N)-90 launched thirteen torpedo planes on a heckler mission over numerous airfields and bases on Kyushu. Lieutenant Charlie Henderson and his crew severely damaged a George fighter but could not confirm it as a kill. As they left the area they encountered a Rufe seaplane and shot it down. Many fires were seen by the crews of the other aircraft, but ground damage could not be confirmed.

On May 13, 1945, bogies were all over the radar screen. At 2145 hours Lieutenant (j.g.) George Oden was launched for a bogie chase. It lasted one hour and fifteen minutes finally paying off in the splash of one Dinah. About an hour later while still under alert, Lieutenant (j.g.) Charles Latrobe was launched, vectored onto a bogie, and splashed one Betty. Meanwhile a thirteen torpedo plane night heckler mission had been launched over Kyushu. Results, one unidentified plane destroyed on the ground with many fires and extensive damage to installations.

Long before dawn on the 14th fifteen fighters were launched. Ten to Kyushu and five over Shikoku. The flight over Kyushu was jumped by three Oscars, and Lieutenant (j.g.) Lamar Harrison was able to destroy one of them. As this unit returned to the task force they found it under attack, and were ordered to orbit until safe to land. Lieutenant (j.g.) George Pete Taylor who was in this group, was vectored onto a Zeke and destroyed it. This would be VF(N)90's last kill. The flight over Shikoku found twenty-five to thirty planes on the ground. Rockets and strafing caused considerable damage to these aircraft, barracks and other installations.

ORDEAL OF THE ENTERPRISE

On May 14th, the USS *Enterprise*, took a direct hit by a Kamikaze on the number one elevator. [6]

Ensign Franklin Goodson describes the nearly catastrophic event:

> "At 0730 a Kamikaze in a Zeke[7] with a 550 pound bomb made a pass over the stern of the *Enterprise* at 4000 feet weaving in and out of the cloud cover that was there. The ship's gunners shot at him and finally he started his dive toward us. I was watching from the cat-walk outside the ready room and was so spelled bound that I couldn't take my eyes off of him.
>
> "As he neared the ship, we swerved to the port side and he did a "split-S" at 200 feet, firing his guns as he crashed into the flight deck of the *Enterprise* at the forward elevator. There was a short delay after he crashed aboard then a tremendous explosion and heavy concussion was felt. I simultaneously dove for cover inside the ready room and never felt the concussion. Two gun mounts had been wiped out near where I stood on the cat walk. On one side of me a gunner was injured seriously and on the other side of me the skipper was knocked out and lay on the deck for a few moments, but recovered.

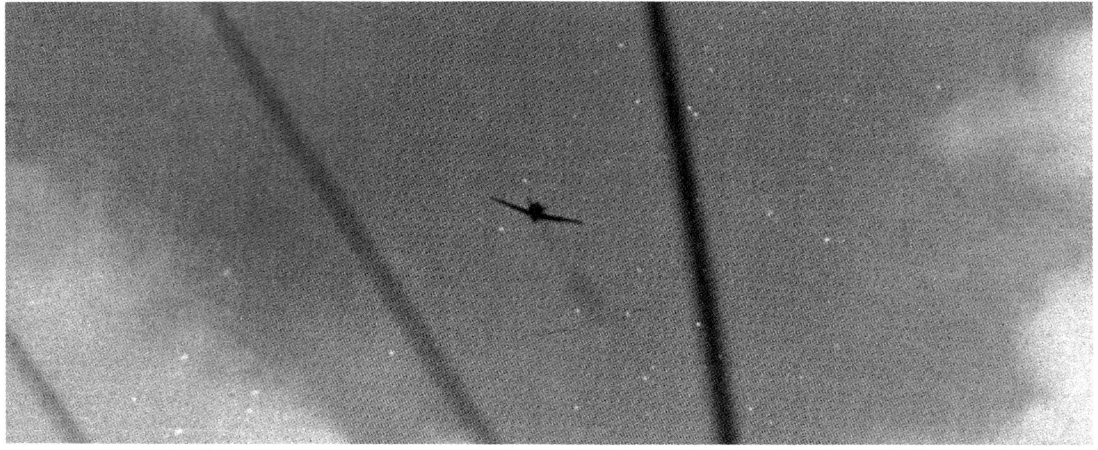

This remarkable sequence, taken through the rigging of *Enterprise* looking aft, shows the approach of a Japanese Kamikaze pilot in a Zeke; he begins to roll his plane; and, upside down, with a 550 pound bomb under the fuselage, he plunges toward the deck of *Enterprise*. (Credit: Bill Balden & Ken Cashen)

"I later discovered thirteen men were killed. Twenty-three planes were destroyed and several men blown over the side. The number one elevator where the Kamikaze hit was blown some 400 feet into the air. The flight deck was warped and burned out in sections, the catapults were severely damaged and of no use. We could neither launch nor recover aircraft, so the crippled *Enterprise* began its long journey home."

The explosive result of the Kamikaze that hit *Enterprise* as seen from the bridge wing of aircraft carrier *Essex*. (Credit: Paul Madden via Rob Roy)

An escort's view of the ordeal of *Enterprise* and the flak filled sky that failed to stop the determined Japanese attacker. (Credit: Bill Barr via MacGlashing)

After the fires were brought under control, this gaping hole, the Number 1 elevator, marked the point of impact of the bomb laden Zeke. (Credit: Bill Barr via MacGlashing)

GOING HOME

The veteran *Enterprise* had fought its last battle. Admiral Mitscher was transferred to the *Randolph*, and we were ordered to return to Ulithi. Many of our fighters had landed on other carriers. Shortly after our return to Ulithi, Wattenburger and Corbit returned from the *Intrepid*; Jones and Truhowsky returned from the *Bennington*; Lieutenant Don Hettwer and Lieutenant (j.g.) Bob Smith from the *Hornet*; Lieutenant (j.g.) Gallant from the *Randolph*; Ensigns Kryshak and Goodson from the *Yorktown*, and Lieutenant (j.g.)s Purcell, Wilmoth and Toffolon also returned from duty on picket destroyers. Enlisted crewmen Linfield and Gary returned, but Bill McKinney was transferred to the *Randolph*. This made VF(N)-90 fairly complete.

However, it was later reported that Lieutenant James Wood, on temporary duty on the *Randolph*, was missing in action. During the attack on the *Enterprise* AMMH1C Robert Riessland of VF(N)-90 had been on the hanger deck when the Zeke hit. The concussion blew him over the side. A number of other men from the ship also were blown over the side. They were picked up by a destroyer and Bob was transferred to the hospital ship USS *Bountiful* with severe burns and other injuries.

We rested in Ulithi from May 19th until May 23rd while our ammunition, was unloaded. At 1400 hours we departed for Uncle Sugar and passed through the Marshall Islands just south of Entiwetok.

At about 0130 on May 28th the ship was buzzed by planes from Night Air Group 91, our relief passing us on the way to take over where we had left off. Night Air Group 90 lost many good men, eleven from the fighter squadron and thirty from the torpedo squadron. VF(N)-90 shot down thirty-seven planes from January 5th to May 14th, some while our pilots were on temporary duty on other carriers. It also destroyed nineteen planes on the ground, seven probables on the ground, and thirty-four damaged aircraft. In all probability others were also destroyed but that could not be determined because of conditions.

Much damage was also inflicted to shipping, railroads, runways, hangars, and barracks. VT(N)-90 shot down five airborne aircraft, destroyed two aircraft on the ground and damaged and probably destroyed several more. Air Group 90 also sank two ships, probably sank two, and damaged eleven others. They also inflicted a lot more damage than could be verified because of the darkness and weather conditions. With periodic time out for repairs and replenishment at Ulithi this is a pretty impressive record.

As Admiral Matt Gardner stated, "Remember men; we were first" referring to Night Air Group 90 being the first defensive/offensive night air carrier unit. May the souls of those comrades we lost both from the squadrons and the ship rest in peace.

Footnotes:

1. On the night of 25 November O'Hare and others, flying from *Enterprise* were tracking Japanese snoopers attempting to hit the Gilbert-Marshall Islands invasion fleet. After an engagement with Japanese Betty bombers O'Hare was missing. Whether his Hellcat was hit by enemy gunners or he succumbed to vertigo remains unknown.

2. In 1943 VF(N)-75 had been deployed on an experimental basis flying F4U Corsairs from bases in the Solomons.

3. P-51 Mustangs of the AAF 15th Fighter Group.

4. The Kawanishi H8K Emily was a huge four-engine flying boat armed with no less than ten guns, five of them 20mm in power driven turrets. Downing this adversary with the two forward firing .50 caliber machine guns of an Avenger was a considerable feat.

5. From the beginning of the Okinawa invasion, April 1st until May 4, 1945 the Japanese Special Attack Corps had expended 655 aircraft in suicide attacks according to Denis & Peggy Warner, THE SACRED WARRIORS, Van Norstrand, 1982. With that effort they had sunk 21 Allied ships of all types and damaged 139.

6. This writer was on the flight deck near the island and about 30 feet back from the elevator. I recall looking over my left shoulder as I was facing the bow of the ship, and seeing the Zeke coming in at us. I thought for sure he was going to hit the Island, but it seemed to turn slightly and dive into the ship. I was blown into the air, coming down and landing on my back and saying "damn it".

I recall getting up and moving to the port side to go down to the ready room to see what if any damage occurred there. It wasn't until hours later that I started feeling pain in my back radiating into my legs.

I was lucky, I could have been closer. We lost thirteen men plus sixty odd wounded.

7. In his book OKINAWA, Penguin-Viking, 1995, author Robert Leckie identifies the Japanese pilot at Lieutenant Tomai Kai. At a mission briefing Leckie says that the orders were: "Get the carriers!" Leckie also records that the bald headed Admiral of the task force, Marc Mitscher, looked at the gaping hole in the *Enterprise* and commented: "If the Japanese keep this up they're going to grow hair on my head yet."

The author of the following is unknown. It has been among John MacGlashing's memorabilia for almost fifty years.Some of the names mentioned are as follows.

Bull Halsey - Admiral William "Bull" halsey
John Sidney - Admiral John S. McCain
Thatch - Captain Jimmy Thatch
Old Mathias - Admiral Matt Gardner
Willing William - Commander William I. Martin
Roscoe From Pasco - Captain Roscoe Newman
Captain Ted - Unknown
The Job For Mac & Kib - LTCDR Robert McCullough VF CO and Russell Kippen Torpedo Squadron CO
Willie Kabler - XO of *Enterprise*

THE NIGHT IS OURS
("LIKEWISE ZERO....ZERO DAYS")

'Twas a dark and stormy night out there
The sea rose masterfully,
And strove to fill with deep despair
The fighting heart of Bull Halsey

"You're helpless on a night like this"
"Who's helpless?" roared the Bull
"Such weather is my favorite dish
I'm glad the moon's not full!"

"Of course my day groups couldn't fly;
Ceiling low and waves too high -
There must be some I could send
To search the seas to the very end."

Then fiery flame from his nostrils blew,
And the gleam did light his eye -
His laughter boomed forth deep and mighty -
"Thank God, there's always Air Group 90!"

Now the fast carrier force of our John Sidney
Was so delighted he ruptured a kidney
With wrinkles smoothed, he turned to Thatch
And said "Jimmy my boy, take a dispatch!"

"Old Mathias is my man,
And Willing William, too
They'll agree to any plan -
To them the sky is always blue!"

Doctrines new were ever spread
By valiant missionaries -
Roscoe from Pasco and Captain Ted
Are now the fleet's night visionaries.

For they're the ones behind the schemes
Who dream these wild fantastic dreams
"Now there's a post I'd like to share"
Mused I, tossed high by their nightmare.

All these oracles to plan
The job for Mac and Kip.
Whose nameless pilots grope to man
Their planes on a darkened ship.

Who cares if this plane won't go,
Engine out - no radio
It's still and "up"; I ought to know
Cause air plot has just old me so.

"Stand by to start the engines on planes of this
Flight - in cockpits busy hands found switches
With never a glimmer of light. "Stand clear of
Propellers" - still thumbs down - "Startengines!
Then Bob's voice was drowned.

Spitting, sputtering engines gasped
Some leaped to instant life,
And a throaty, thundering roar at last
Engaged the wind's bold blast in strife.

Taxi down a wave washed desk
And give your mags a careful check -
There's someone there knee deep in brine -
Neptune Rex, with wands that shine.

Left brake, right brake, tail wheel locked -
Forward, backward - let the ship rock!
Blinking lights say your're in the gear -
Lord - I must have been trying for a year!

Unperturbed by aircraft missions,
Willie Kabler stands -
Starting his brooms and setting conditions,
Keeping house as best he can.

Wings spread, flaps down - one look around
Isn't there some way to give it a down?
There's the wind-up - give'er the gun -
Lights on - head back - and a 60 foot run.

Wrhrump! You gasp, and strain for the wheels.
Altitude, gyro, airspeed, heading -
Believe what they tell you,
Not how it feels.

Just below, the wild waves leap,
Licking their chops hungrily
Maybe I do have 300 feet -
But they look awfully close, to me!

A cylinder misses, your're due for a splash
Why worry - after all,
You'll be picked up in just a flash
Says Captain G.B.H. (to us "Bud") Hall

One look outside - Lord it's black -
I sure wish I were back in the sack.
Where are the others? Rendezvous, Hell!
If I keep from spinning in I'm doing Damn well.

What was the message from Com 3rd Fleet?
"The night is yours - Good Luck - Godspeed -
The prize is there - go grab it -"
Secretly, I think he added -
"Frankly brother - you can have it!"

(Above) The staff officers of Night Air Group 90, Comdr. Bill Martin is third from the left. (Credit: MacGlashing)

(Right) William Martin, pioneer in night carrier operations and CO of Air Group 90, retired as a Vice Admiral. (Credit: USNI)

Officer and enlisted aircrews of VT(N)-90. (Credit: MacGlashing)

Enlisted personnel of VT(N)-90. (Credit: MacGlashing)

Officers of VF(N)-90. (Credit: MacGlashing)

Enlisted personnel of VF(N)-90. (Credit: MacGlashing)

APPENDIX A
ROSTER OF AIR GROUP 90

Air Group Commanders Staff:
Commander William I. Martin
Lieutenant Comander Edwin G. Hurlburt, flight surgeon
Lieutenant Comander William B. Chase
Lieutenant William B. Emmons
Lieutenant (j.g.) Hugh J. Karr, Jr.
Lieutenant (j.g.) Albert A. Stephan
Lieutenant (j.g.) Edwin R. Jenks
ARM1C Robert K. Barnett
CPHOM Harold T. Gholson
ACRT Robert W. Grenier
CY Anthony Schillaci

Night Fighter Squadron 90:
Lieutenant Comander Robert J. McCullough, CO
Lieutenant. Nelson V. Phillips, XO
Lieutenant Robert E. Shields
Lieutenant. Harry S. Rodgers
Lieutenant Philip Horr, Jr.
Lieutenant. Russell D. Otis
Lieutenant Kenneth D. Smith
Lieutenant. John R. Woolford
Lieutenant Carl S. Nielsen
Lieutenant. Owen D. Young
Lieutenant Arthur W. Edwards
Lieutenant. Donald F. Hettwer
Lieutenant Raymond E.Weathers
Lieutenant Dallas E. Runion
Lieutenant (j.g.) W. I. Gille
Lieutenant (j.g.) Logan T. MacMillan
Lieutenant (j.g.) Raymond N. Vranicar
Lieutenant (j.g.) Robert E. Pruitt
Lieutenant (j.g.) John A. Thoerle
Lieutenant (j.g.) Wallace G. Campbell
Lieutenant (j.g.) William G. Piscopo
Lieutenant (j.g.) Leonard W. Wilmoth
Lieutenant (j.g.) Richard I. Jones
Lieutenant (j.g.) John E. Toffolon
Lieutenant (j.g.) Robert C. Wattenburger
Lieutenant (j.g.) Lamar F. Harrison
Lieutenant (j.g.) Frank J. Truhowsky
Lieutenant (j.g.) Stanley P. Kurant
Lieutenant (j.g.) Wesley R. Williams
Lieutenant (j.g.) Layton E. Robison
Lieutenant (j.g.) James P. Purcell
Lieutenant (j.g.) Rex D. Milton
Lieutenant (j.g.) John R. Kenyon, Jr.
Lieutenant (j.g.) Arthur P. Kegelman
Lieutenant (j.g.) Kenneth D. Close
Lieutenant (j.g.) Raymond R. Chase, Jr.
Lieutenant (j.g.) Mark A. Yorston
Lieutenant (j.g.) George p. Taylor
Lieutenant (j.g.) Will J. Squires
Lieutenant (j.g.) James F. Loveridge
Lieutenant (j.g.) George H. Lockwood
Lieutenant (j.g.) Robert T. Corbit
Lieutenant (j.g.) Charles R. Latrobe
Lieutenant (j.g.) George A. Oden
Lieutenant (j.g.) John W. Cole
Lieutenant (j.g.) Charles W. Horne
Lieutenant (j.g.) Leonard T. Skreba
Lieutenant (j.g.) Joseph C. Gallant
Lieutenant (j.g.) Arthur Hansen
Lieutenant (j.g.) Glen R. Earl
Lieutenant (j.g.) George E. Franklin
Lieutenant (j.g.) Robert J. Smith
Lieutenant (j.g.) Harold S. Durfee
Ensign Joseph Donchess
Ensign Joseph F. Sowar
Ensign Joseph E. Wall
Ensign Franklin T. Goodson
Ensign James R. Perkins
Ensign Waldo W. West
Ensign R. I. Rodenmyer
ACMM Theodore E. Donnan
ACOM William J. Anderson
ACRM Arthur J. Burgh
AMM1C Harry N. Barbouletos
ARM1C Bernard H. Boskamp, Jr.
ARM2C Charles L. Brubaker
ART1C William J. Byrne
AMM2C Mario A. Capulli
ART1C Keith E. Clayson
ARM3C John F. Cooligan
ART1C Emerson Elder
ART1C Earle L. Faupell
PR1C George Gallagher
ART1C Leon H. Gary
AOM2C Overton T. Green
RDM3C John A. Grosskopf
RT3C Daniel J. Hamiliton
ART1C William G. Heise
RDM2C Edward F. Hoberhouer
ARM2C Joseph J. Hrosak
AMM1C Robert V. Krakauskas
RDM3C Don C. Kirk
AOM1C Harry A. Leonard
ART1C Robert F. Linfield
ART1C William F. Lord
Y1C John W. Mac Glashing
AOM1C Ralph R. Marsh
RDM3C Jerome H. Marek
AMM1C Martin F. Marnik
AM1C Joseph S. Maxim
RDM3C George H. Myers
ART1C William I. McKinney
ARM2C John J. McNerney
ART1C Jack E. Nolde
ARM1C Vincent P. Olivieri

ART1C Arnold W. Olson
ART1C Martin L. Pebler
ART1C Leon E. Riemer
ART1C Arthur M. Rhodes
RT2C Richard D. Rossman
ART1C Edwin E. Scharath
AMMH1C Robert F. Riessland
AOM2C William Scruta
RDM3C Adrian R. Stone
ART1C Arthur P. Summers
ART1C John M. Sunderson
AEM1C Leroy G. Thomas
AMM2C Byrl F. Trostel
RDM3C Wyatt C. Urton
AMM1C Evan O. Willis

Night Torpedo Squadron 90:
Lieutenant Charles E. Henderson, CO
Lieutenant James S. Moore, XO
Lieutenant William D. Bacon
Lieutenant Joseph A. Doyle, Jr.
Lieutenant Ralph W. Cummings
Lieutenant Edward Hidalgo
Lieutenant Robert R. Jones
Lieutenant James W. Plummer
Lieutenant (J.G.) Ernest J. Lawton, Jr.
Lieutenant (J.G.) Shannon McCrary
Lieutenant (J.G.) Gilbert S. Blake
Lieutenant (J.G.) Clifton R. Largess, Jr.
Lieutenant (J.G.) Herbert T. Wade
Lieutenant (J.G.) William B. Balden, Jr.
Lieutenant (J.G.) William R. Thomas
Lieutenant (J.G.) George W. Bruel
Lieutenant (J.G.) Charles E. Gerbron
Lieutenant (J.G.) George E. McLaughlin
Lieutenant (J.G.) Joseph W. Jewell, Jr.
Lieutenant (J.G.) Edwin H. Halbach
Lieutenant (J.G.) Charles E. Brooks
Lieutenant (J.G.) Robert B. Hadley
Lieutenant (J.G.) William L. Cromley
Lieutenant (J.G.) Lavern F. McLaughlin
Lieutenant (J.G.) Joseph M. Scarborough
Lieutenant (J.G.) Robert S. Heid
Lieutenant (J.G.) Zane E. Carey
Lieutenant (J.G.) Joseph F. Jennings
Lieutenant (J.G.) Henry G. Hinrichs
Lieutenant (J.G.) John M. Ashton
Lieutenant (J.G.) Ralph A. Turpin
Ensign James D. Landon
Ensign Robert Roy
Ensign Knox O. Scott
Ensign James A. Blazek
Ensign Wallace W. Denhoff
ACOM Jesse T. Boatwright
ACMM John H. Cirillo
ACRM Ralph A. Gowling
ACM Rexford B. Holmgrin
ACRM Herman R. Ludwig
ACOM Raymond D. Martin
ACRM Joseph F. McMullen
ACRT George F. Pheiffer, Jr.
ACMM Daniel B. Ryan, Jr.
ACMM Leland F. Sturla
ACOM William J. Thornton
ACRM Thomas T. Watts
PR1C Alvin C. Adams
ARM2C Robert H. Brecount
ARM2C John A. Albrich, Jr.
ARM3C Thurmal L. Armstrong
ARM3C Charles J. Baker
ARM3C Fred H. Bargetzi
ARM2C Edward J. Boland
ARM3C Frank G. Camidge
AMM2C Everett E. Caswell
ARM3C Edward W. Cobb
AOM1C Borge W. Dahl
AOM3C Charles J. Dalton, Jr.
ARM3C Thomas E. Davidson
AOM3C John D. Davis
ARM3C John R. Deal
ART1C John H. Evans
Y1C John H. Fields
ARM2C Stanley E. Francis
ARM3C Robert A. Gerth
ARM2C William A. Griffin
AOM2C Mayo Grubb
ARM3C Everett L. Gruelle
ARM1C Frank E. Gunn
ARM2C Thomas M. Henderson
ARM3C Lawrence D. Holaday
AOM3C John A. Hotchkiss
ARM1C Joseph Hranek
ARM3C Carl D. Jones
ARM1C William R. Kiser
ARM1C James B. Kitchen
ART2C Elmer W. L. Krock
AEM1C Regis J. Kujava
ART1C Gordon S. La Boundy
ARM1C Joseph D. Lindsey
ARM3C Elwood L. Littlefield
ARM3C Robert L. Lundfelt
AMM1C Henry R. May
AMM1C William O. Mefford
AOM2C Daniel J. Mc Hale
ARM2C Fred J. Meny
AOM1C Philip H. Morgan
AOM1C Armando Nelson
ARM2C George H. Newcomb
ARM2C Oliver K. Ohlund
AMM1C John R. Peterson
ARM3C Roy J. Pintacura
AMM1C Irving L. Poritzky
ARM2C Leonard Prym
ARM2C Le Roy A. Pulliam
ARM3C John D. Rockafellow
AMM1C Raymond Roundy

ARM2C Arnold C. Rouse, Jr.
ARM3C Michael C. Ryan
ARM3C Gerald B. Schneider
AOM3C Carl H. Seidel
ARM1C Harry R. Shaw
ARM1C Marvin E. Smith
AMM2C Peter G. Smith
ART1C Seymour Solomon
ARM3C Edmund Statkewicz
ARM2C Arthur W. Teets
ART1C Waliter C. Tessmer
ART1C John A. Volpe
ART1C Donald L. Warner, Jr.
ARM3C Eugene A. Wengler
ART2C William B. Yerrick

Inadvertently some names may have been omitted.

APPENDIX B

Personnel Fatalities Of Night Air Group 90 From August 1944 - May 1945

VF(N)-90

Ensign Richard Blake Jones, Barbers Point, August 31, 1944
Ensign John Frank Lungershausen, Barbers Point, November10, 1944
Ensign Charles William Gibson, MIA at sea, January 7, 1945
Ensign John Gary Sowell, MIA at sea, January 7, 1945
Lieutenant (j.g.) Robert Franklin Wright, MIA Hong Kong area, January 16, 1945
Ensign Erwin Garner Nash, MIA at sea, January 16, 1945
Ensign William Leroy Sadler, MIA at sea, February 10, 1945
Ensign Fred Allen Hunziker, MIA Okinawa area, April13, 1945
Lieutenant James J. Wood, MIA Okinawa area, May 2, 1945
Lieutenant (j.g.)James Trowbridge Tucker, MIA at sea, May 9, 1945

VT(N)-90

Ensign James Joseph Murphy, Barbers Point, October 15, 1944
Ensign Charles William Barton, Barbers Point, October 18, 1944
ARM3C Kenneth Harry Ramsey, Barbers Point, October 18, 1944
ARM3C James Comstock Hayes, Barbers Point, October 18, 1944
Ensign James Lawrence Crane, Barbers Point, November 20, 1944
ARM3C Manion George Herlofsen, Barbers Point, November 20, 1944
ARM3C Nick Curnich, MIA at sea, December 26, 1944
Lieutenant (j.g.) Eugene Ralph Lee, MIA at sea, December 29, 1944
ARM1C Manford Lyle Cooney, MIA at sea, January 15, 1945
ARM3C Mervin Leroy Porter, MIA at sea, January 15, 1945
ARM3C Robert Lewis Brought, of injuries received on deck crash, 1/15/45
Lieutenant Russell Ford Kippen, MIA Formosa, January 22, 1945
Lieutenant (j.g.) Uri Alexander Munro, MIA Formosa, January 22, 1945
ARM1C Paul Adrian Floyd, MIA Formosa, January 22, 1945
Lieutenant (j.g.) Chester Gilbert Keep, MIA Formosa, January 22, 1945
AMM2C Guy Beevers, MIA Formosa, January 22, 1945
ARM3C Dale Robert Lieberenz, MIA Formosa, January 22, 1945
Ensign John Preston Wood, MIA Formosa, January 22, 1945
ARM3C John Howard Findley, MIA Formosa, January 22, 1945
ARM3C Richard James Hall, MIA Formosa, January 22, 1945
ARM3C William Dennis Crowley, MIA at sea, January 25, 1945
Ensign John Whitney Stuckey, MIA at sea, February 17, 1945
ARM3C James Clark Eldred, MIA at sea, Februay 17, 1945
AOM3C Victor George Chaney, MIA at sea, February 17, 1945
Lieutenant C. B. Collins, MIA at sea, February 22, 1945
Lieutenant (j.g.) Robert Scott Gowdy, MIA at sea, February 22, 1945
ARM2C Ferris Ivory, MIA at sea, February 22, 1945
Lieutenant (j.g.) George Harrell Atkinson, MIA at sea, March 15, 1945
ARM2C Ernest Robert Magalotti, MIA at sea, March 15, 1945
ARM3C Norvel Preston Moss, MIA at sea, March 15,

APPENDIX C
AIR TO AIR VICTORY CLAIMS

PILOT	DESTROYED-PROBABLE-DAMAGED
VF(N)-90:	
Lt. Carl S. Nielsen	3-0-0
Lt. (j.g.) Robert C. Wattenburger	2-0-0
Lt. James J. Wood	3-0-0
Lt. (j.g.) Wesley R. Williams	1-0-0
Lt. Kenneth D. Smith [1.]	5-0-1
Ens. Glen R. Earl	1-0-0
Lt. (j.g.) James P. Purcell, Jr.	0-1-0
Lt. (j.g.) William G. Piscopo[2.]	1-0-0
Lt. (j.g.) Will. J. Squires	2-0-0
Ens. James R. Perkins	1-1-0
Lt. (j.g.) Lamar F. Harrison	1.5-0-0
Lt. (j.g.) Layton E. Robison	.5-0-0
Lt. Dallas E. Runion	2-0-0
Lt. (j.g.) Joseph C. Gallant	1-0-0
Lt. Owen D. Young	4.5-0-0
Lt. (j.g.) John R. Kenyon, Jr.	1-0-0
Ens. Waldo W. West[3.]	3-0-0
Lt. (j.g.) George A. Oden	1-0-0
Lt. (j.g.) Charles H. Latrobe	2.5-0-0
Lt. (j.g.) George P. Taylor	1-0-0
Totals	37-2-1

Note: Conditions sometimes caused *Enterprise* crews to land on other carriers in their task force and then to conduct operations there until able to return to their ship.

1. K.D. Smith scored two kills and one damage while flying from *Bennington.*
2. William Piscopo scored one victory while flying from *Bennington.*
3. Waldo West scored three kills while flying from *Bunker Hill.*

Lt. (j.g.) Arthur Hansen claimed two victories during previous service with VF(N)-41

VT(N)-90

Lt. Charles E. Henderson, III	2-1-0
Lt. (j.g.) Edwin H. Halbach	
ARM2c Thomas M. Henderson	
Lt. (j.g.) Clifton R. Largess, Jr.	2-0-0
ARM1c John C. Sullivan	
ARM2c Stanley E. Francis	
Lt. Ralph W. Cummings	1-0-0
Lt. (j.g.) Zane E. Carey	
ARM1c Joseph D. Lindsey	
Totals	5-1-0

Source: Frank Olynyk, USN Credits for the Destruction of Enemy Aircraft in Air-to-Air Combat, World War II.

APPENDIX D
U.S. NAVY NIGHT AIR UNIT AERIAL VICTORY CLAIMS:

SQ/AIR GROUP	YEAR	CARRIER	CLAIMS
VF(N)-41	1944	*Independence*	46-3-3
VF(N)-75	1943	Solomons*	7-2-0
VF(N)-76	1944	*Hornet*	37-2-0
VF(N)-77	1944	*Essex*	8-0-0
VF(N)-78	1944	*Intrepid*	2-0-2
Air Group 90	1945	*Enterprise*	42-3-1
VF(N)-91	1945	*Bon Homme Richard*	9-2-0
VF(N)-101	1944	*Intrepid*	5-1-3

* Shore Based

Source: Frank Olynyk, USN Credits for the Destruction of Enemy Aircraft in Air-to-Air Combat, World War II.

DEFINITIVE MILITARY AVIATION HISTORY

FROM PHALANX

The Gold Wings Series

Navy and Marine Unit and Battle Histories

No. 1. **Wildcats Over Casablanca** by J. W. Lambert $11.95

No. 2 . **Sundowners:** VF-11 in WW II by Barrett Tillman $12.95

No. 3. **Marine Mitchells:** PBJ Operations in the Pacific by Jerry Scutts $12.95

No. 4. **Carrier Battle in the Philippine Sea** by Barrett Tillman $12.95

No. 5. **Fantail Fighters** by Jerry Scutts $12.95

No. 6. **Batmen**: Night Air Group 90 in WW II by John MacGlashing $12.95

Pending Titles:

The Destruction of MAG 22 (Midway, June 1942) by Robert J. Cressman

Gold Wings Over Fortress Europe by Steven D. Hill

VMF-223 at Guadalcanal by John Lundstrom

All monographs in the Gold Wings Series contain **color profiles** by **John Valo**.

These monographs contain combat history that has been glossed over by the larger works. Fine text, accompanied by personal experiences, are augmented by **rare photos**, **maps** and lush **appendices**.